Celebrating the Sacraments

VERITAS

First published 1996 by
Veritas Publications
7-8 Lower Abbey Street
Dublin 1

Copyright © Colm Kilcoyne 1996

ISBN 1 85390 300 0

The numbers in parenthesis throughout the text refer to the paragraphs of the *Catechism of the Catholic Church*, copyright © (in Ireland) 1994 Veritas Publications – Libreria Editrice Vaticana. All rights reserved.

Cover design by Bill Bolger
Printed in Ireland by Paceprint Ltd, Dublin

The Jews have a story about the moment that God creates Adam. Immediately, Adam looks at God and asks: 'Who am I?'

Ever since, from cradle to grave, this is still the question, the driving force that gives energy to all we do. Everything we do is a search for an answer. 'Who am I?'

The answer comes in drips and drabs. In moments that seem to say: 'Stay with me now and I'll whisper you secrets. Listen closely and you'll find clues to your questions'.

I see the sacraments as such moments. They freeze time and insert meaning.

There is the story of the King of northern England who in 627 AD was resisting Christianity. An adviser is supposed to have said to him: 'Your majesty, when you sit at table with your lords and vassals, in the winter when the fire burns warm and bright on the hearth and the storm is howling outside, bringing snow and the rain, it happens of a sudden that a little bird flies into the hall. For the few moments that it is inside the hall it doesn't feel the cold, but as soon as it leaves your sight, it returns to the dark of winter. We do not know what went before and we do not know what follows. If the new doctrine can speak surely of these things, it is well for us to follow it'. *(A New Catechism,* Herder and Herder)

The sacraments are those moments when the little bird of wisdom flies into our questions. They connect us with what went before and what is to come. They waken mystery.

I find this quote helpful; 'A sacrament is a festive action in which Christians assemble to celebrate their lived experience and to call to heart their common story. The action is a symbol of God's care for us in Christ. Enacting the symbol brings us close to one another in the church and to the Lord who is there... (*Tad Guize: The Book of Sacramental Basics,* Paulist Press)

Anne Frank wrote in her diary: 'Today the sun is shining, the sky is a deep blue, there is a lovely breeze and I am longing – so longing – for everything.'

Richard Bach wrote in Jonathan Livingstone Seagull: 'I am not sure this planet is home. They have funny customs here but I'm fond of this place. There's a magnet pulling me against the fence of this world limits. I have a strange feeling that we have come from the other side of the fence'.

The sacraments are magnets pulling us against the limits of our understanding. The water, oils, candles, bread, wine – ordinary things telling us an extraordinary story – that God so loved the world that in the fullness of time he sent his Son to be our Saviour.

The words – ordinary words telling us that the Word was made flesh and lives among us.

The symbols – it is celebration, not doctrine, that lies at the heart of religion. Our faith didn't start with concepts but with experiences. Symbols were used to celebrate those experiences. The disciples on the road to Emmaus first had the experience of the Risen Christ and then celebrated it in the breaking of bread.

The touches – ordinary touches that tell us that this world has been touched by the breath of God and that the shadow of his Son's cross and empty tomb falls over all the earth and will give meaning to our questions if we will sit quiet before the mystery.

That is the key word. Mystery. Transcendence.

The liturgical celebration involves signs and symbols relating to creation (candles, water, fire), human life (washing, anointing, breaking bread) and the history of salvation (the rites of the Passover) ... These cosmic elements, human rituals, and gestures of remembrance of God become bearers of the saving and sanctifying action of Christ (1189).

I lived in Achill for a while. The Minaun cliffs are down the island, a marvellous sheer drop into the sea. At that time, some people from faraway places like Dublin were coming to Achill at weekends for hang-gliding. It was new at the time.

I was in a house one day and the woman of the house told me she was very worried that her middle-aged husband was losing the run of himself and wanted to take up hang-gliding. She felt he was displaying the foolishness of a child wanting to play with fire.

I was careful not to take sides so I'm afraid she dismissed me and told me I was no great help in her fight to bring her man to his senses.

Later I met himself. He had been told about my weak refusal to take sides. By now, I had the courage to tell him that I thought what he had in mind was bordering on the foolish.

He brought me to a window and showed me the ruins of an old house and stables across the road. He told me about the man who lived there alone, years ago. This man used to get my friend, when he was a child, to tidy the house, bring in the turf and generally straighten up for him.

He had a scraggy pony. No reins, no nothing. The reward was that the boy could ride the pony, bareback, around the small field, when the jobs were done.

Like the Garden of Eden, there was a clause. On no account was he to jump the stone wall at the end of the field.

This day, when the boy was teetering on the edge of childhood and young boyhood, he did the messages as usual. He remembers what happens next. 'I got up on the pony and started a trot around the field. Then a bit of a gallop. I saw the forbidden wall and slowly I pulled the pony into the corner furthest from the wall. I gave him a good tip with my shoe. He took off. We came to the wall. There was no turning back. I gave a shout. He rose. We went over the wall. My seat left him. I was airborne, for a few seconds. It was unbelievable. I felt I was straining against something new and strange in life.'

'I have been haunted by that moment. Ever since, I have wanted to recreate it. I haven't. And I feel I'd get it from hang-gliding.'

The hunger for transcendence. The ache for meaning. The sacraments are moments when that ache is heard and the hunger fed. They are moments when we touch mystery. They are places where we will find answers to the question: 'Who am I?'

That man never let life eclipse mystery. Unfortunately it can and does happen. When it does, the sacraments lose their flavour. They are seen as some kind of magic performed by druids.

I was in a house. I had taken off my collar. The young boy of the house, aged maybe eight, came in, saw the collar, tucked it under his chin and went around the kitchen ordering: 'Stand up! Sit down! Give me money!'

What this boy was experiencing in the sacrament of the Eucharist was a string of things happening, with no thread of meaning holding them together. Talk about the eclipse of mystery, the hunger for transcendence. Maybe he was too young. Maybe not.

The French bishops said some time ago that *good liturgy enhances faith, poor celebration weakens it.* There is no such thing as a neutral sacrament. It is either revealing meaning or blocking it. The sacraments are the healing presence of Christ. For this presence to be experienced, participants need faith, a degree of elegance and a respect for mystery.

THE SACRAMENTS OF CHRISTIAN INITIATION

The Sacrament of Baptism

We had a water font in the hall, near the door. When we were going out to anything half important, my mother always drowned us in holy water and warned us: 'And don't forget who you are'.

I never asked what she meant. I'd like to think she drew her remarks from the holy water. That she was reminding us that we were 'a new creation and had clothed ourselves in Christ'. She was telling us to 'bring that dignity unstained into the everlasting life of heaven'.

Somewhere along the line, she had been taught the link between holy water and Baptism. Taught that it is not a static pond from which we were splashed years ago, but a living stream meant to refresh us every day. We are to wear the mark of Chrism in our hearts long after it has dried on our foreheads.

Since the beginning of the world, water, so humble and wonderful a creature, has been the source of life and fruitfulness.... At the very dawn of creation, your Spirit breathed on the waters, making them the wellspring of all holiness. (1218)

I know of no way to talk about Baptism other than the way William Bausch speaks of it in *A New Look at the Sacraments* (23rd Publications).

He journeys with Mark, a young Roman way back when the Church was young. Mark is twenty-six, restless, searching for meaning. He meets a Christian, another young man, who agrees to be his sponsor. For three years this man is Mark's sponsor and tutors him in prayer, instruction and, importantly, the witness of his own life.

Now, it is the beginning of Lent, make your mind up time for Mark. He decides to hand in his name for Baptism.

On the day before Lent begins, the presbyter writes down the names of all.... On the day when Lent begins, the bishop's chair is set up in the middle of the great church.... The bishop one by one asks of the sponsors if the candidates are free from vice.

Mark gets the nod and the bishop writes down his name in the baptismal register. A big moment.

For the next seven weeks, Mark learns that the Christian life is made up of choices. He studies key gospel passages.

First week: The Temptations in the desert. He learns that we are worth only the value of our ideals – when the chips are down, only conviction pulls you through. The soul wins freedom only when it chooses to face down temptation.

Second week: The Transfiguration. 'Lord, it is good for us to be here.' Mark learns that it is better to see 'being here' as a stage on the way to joining Jesus in glory. The choice is between making tents here or living in God's mansion for eternity.

Third week: The Samaritan woman at the well.

The choice between endless thirst and living water, between flimsy worship of tired gods and true worship of the one God.

Fourth week: The blind man. Christ is the light of the world. He gives sight to the blind man. Now, the Pharisees are the blind ones. Will Mark open his eyes to see the light of Christ? His choice.

Fifth week: The story of Lazarus. Marvellous stuff. Mark is really getting down to it now. He is learning about community – he whom you love is sick; about the humanity of Jesus – Jesus wept; about the Father of life working through his Son – Lazarus, come forth. The choice for Mark is between 'a life of death' and a life through which he lets the power of Jesus flow.

Mark reaches Holy Week. On Holy Thursday he takes a bath for ritual purification. On Good Friday and Holy Saturday he fasts and prays.

On Holy Saturday night, the bishop, the sponsors, Mark and the rest of the candidates are in a darkened room.

The ceremony begins. The candidates face west towards the setting sun, darkness, death, the evil one.

Mark stretches out his hands. 'I detach myself from you Satan, from your pomp, your worship, and your angels'.

About face towards the East and the rising sun, towards light, life, Christ the light of the world.

Mark stretches out his hands. 'I attach myself to you, O Christ!' This is choice, conversion.

The bishop comes to Mark and anoints his head with oil. Being sealed for Christ as a shepherd marks his own sheep. The master, his slaves.

Into a pre-chamber to the womb/tomb shaped baptistery. 'Unless you are born again of water and the Holy Spirit you cannot be saved.'

By now, it is almost midnight on Holy Saturday night. Mark steps into the water. The bishop puts his hand on Mark's head. Time to make his big choice. Mark ducks his head under. When he comes up the bishop asks: 'Do you believe in the Father?' 'Yes'. Down and up again. 'Do you believe in the Son? Do you believe in the Holy Spirit?' 'Yes, Yes!'

The bishop baptises Mark in the name of the Father, Son and Holy Spirit. His five senses are anointed with Chrism.

The anointing with Chrism shows that the person who has become a Christian, is, one 'anointed' by the Holy Spirit, and incorporated into Christ who is anointed priest, prophet and king. (1241)

Mark is then robed in white linen, handed a lighted candle and given the kiss of peace.

Mark is a Christian. He walks with the other new Christians from the baptistery to the cathedral to take part, for the first time, in the full Eucharist.

According to the Apostle Paul, the believer enters through Baptism into communion with Christ's death, is buried with him, and rises with him. The baptised have 'put on Christ' (Gal 3:27). (1227)

Before I die, I would love to walk the path Mark walked. To take the time to relearn that the Christian life is a series of choices between west and east, darkness and light, death and life, evil and Christ. To touch the symbols with new senses – water, oil, fresh cloth, lighted candles, the kiss of peace. After all that, to walk into a Eucharist as if for the very first time. Mystery.

The Sacrament of Confirmation
I had a terrible Confirmation day. A parcel arrived from America from an aunt, to dress Colm for the big day. Out came a little velvet black jacket and a big red bow to tie on the arm.

Nowadays, children wear anything. In my time, it was either a brown gansey or a navy blue gansey. Definitely not a little velvet black jacket with a big red bow to tie on the arm.

I made a tame protest but I got short shrift. I'd wear it and be glad to have it and I'd write a short note to my aunt to say how much I appreciated her kind gift and how much admired the jacket was.

I wore it. It was cruelty from start to finish. Sixty odd children mocked and scoffed. I was mortified. The only thing, this was pre video and pre the camera craze. No record of my humiliation exists, except in my tender memory.

I know all about Confirmation making us soldiers of Christ. I had to fight to survive that day.

Baptism, the Eucharist and Confirmation together make up 'the sacraments of Christian initiation'. Somehow, Confirmation loses out to the other two. Partly, I suspect because we seem less familiar with the work of the Holy Spirit. Confirmation is the anointing with the Holy Spirit.

There are two main images of the Holy Spirit in the Bible. Water and air. The living water that restores parched earth, animals and humans. And the air, either the gentle breath or the violent storm.

Both images help us understand Confirmation.

It is usual to say that the symbolism of water is lost on us here. That we get too much of it to appreciate the way nature and people gasp when it is absent. Well, the summer of '95 may have taught us. Rivers dried up, pets were distressed, grass got burnt, fields lay panting under the blue skies and we drank water by the gallon. We learnt about drought.

The Holy Spirit refreshes parched souls. Where there is aridity, the Spirit brings awe and wonder, where there is weakness, the Spirit coaxes fullness of life, where there is timidity, the Spirit causes courage. The gifts of the Holy Spirit.

The second image is of air, either the gentle breath that whispers love, forgiveness and encouragement, or the storm that disrupts, tosses in the air and rearranges our plans. The breath that moved over the deep at creation. The Pentecost that heralded a new creation.

On Pentecost Sunday the disciples were timid, fearful. They felt alone without Jesus. The Spirit came. The tongues of fire were like our Chrism. An anointing with the gifts of the Holy Spirit.

> By this anointing, the confirmand receives the 'mark', the seal of the Holy Spirit. A seal is a symbol of a person, a sign of personal authority, or ownership of an object...This seal of the Holy Spirit marks our total belonging to Christ, our enrolment in his service forever.... (1295, 1296)

Confirmation is one of the three Sacraments of Christian initiation. The ceremony brings that out.

> When Confirmation is celebrated separately from Baptism, its connection with Baptism is expressed, among other ways, by the renewal of baptismal promises. The celebration of Confirmation during the Eucharist helps underline the unity of the sacraments of Christian initiation. (1321)

The Sacrament of the Eucharist

The day the circus came to town, a few us us who lived near the Fairgreen were always let off school. It was a custom. We did messages for the circus people – milk and bread from the shops. Mostly, though, we sat on the Fairgreen wall and watch them put up the marquee.

It was a ritual with very little text. Men with tattoos swung sledge hammers, pulled ropes, stretched canvas, placed poles on the ground like knives and forks at a meal.

They looped ropes through rings on the canvas. Drove pegs. In the middle of it all they dug a hole and laid a huge pole on the ground, its bottom tip inches away from the hole.

It looked a mess, a chaotic collection of bits and pieces. A man stood near the hole in the middle of the confusion, sledge hammer at the ready.

The gaffer gave a shout. Everywhere, workers pulled on ropes. The short poles straighted up and hauled the canvas with them. The huge pole in the middle took the strain and groaned almost upright. But not quite.

There came a moment when they could get no more movement from the ropes, the poles or the canvas. It was then that the man in the middle, with the sledge hammer came into his own. He'd spit on his hands, hit the bottom of the main pole and sink it into the hole. The pole would shudder, steady and stop.

That was the minute the whole web of ropes, canvas and poles took shape. Ropes tightened. Canvas lost its slack. The contours filled out. Before our eyes had risen the wonder of the child's world: a circus marquee.

Then they'd let us walk into the marquee. That was magic. To stand in the peculiar light that green canvas lets through. To smell the grass already sweating and the fascination of the main pole. The thing that held it all together.

Later, when I had the usual questions about what

Mass was about, the marquee in the Fairgreen came back to me. I had problems seeing how all the pieces fitted. I longed for some truth that held it together.

I think I see it now. Holding it together is Jesus Christ. His is the presence that gives it shape and meaning.

Short of understanding that, I'd be in trouble. I'd be looking too hard at the quality of the music, the diction of the readers, the shape of the vestments, the quality of the sermon. All these matter, but what matters most is that this is a coming into the presence of Jesus Christ. Once I get that right, the rest is a bonus when it is well done, an irritation when it is poor.

> The mode of Christ's presence under the Eucharistic species is unique. It raises the Eucharist above all the sacraments as 'the perfection of the spiritual life and the end to which all the sacraments tend.' (1374)

Christ is present in four ways in the Eucharist. In the priest presiding, in the people gathered, in the word read and in the bread broken.

1. The priest presiding

His task at Mass is to release meaning. To let God be active in his people. In the gospel, the curious said, 'Sir, we would see Jesus?' (Jn 12:20-21). Adam's question – 'Who am I?' – in another form.

Vatican II says: 'The ministry itself is the prime source of the priest's spirituality. It is the same word which interprets the priest's life and the life of the people.'

Which means that the priest's own life is meant to be Eucharistic. Or redemptive, if that means more to you. Either way he is called to belief that in the midst of all this history, at a thousand different times and places, in a thousand forms, the one thing that occurs that produces and sustains it all is the Silent Coming of God. The pole holding it all together. Like the ark of the covenant which the wandering Jews pulled to the centre of their camp each night, the priest must see in the Eucharist the tabernacle which defines who he and the people are.

To be a celebrant challenges the priest at the level of his humanity and of his faith. This is not easy. Morris West wrote, in *The Shoes of the Fisherman:* 'It costs so much to be a full human being. One has to abandon altogether the search for security, and reach out to the risk of living with both arms, one has to embrace the world like a lover. One has to accept pain as a condition of existence.'

The celebrant is a translator. In *Philadelphia Here I Come,* Brian Friel has Gar talking to the parish priest: 'You could translate all this dreadful bloody buffoonery into Christian terms that will make life bearable to us all. Why arid, Canon? Isn't it your job to translate "Why don't you speak then?"' The challenge set by every congregation.

2. In the people gathered
Cyril Cusack had a prayer he said just as he went on

stage: 'Dear Lord, help me to remember I didn't write the blessed thing.' A prayer about subservience. Of not being in the way. Of staying alert to the fact that Mass is Christ present and active in and with his people. Of letting people experience the movement of Christ's healing power in their lives.

'I feel sorry for these people because they have been with me for three days and now have nothing to eat. I don't want to send them away without feeding them, for they might faint on their way home.'

The tenderness which people should experience at Mass. The feeding of their hungers. The glimpse of the Transfiguration. The washing of tired feet.

This is why the Eucharist is linked to Baptism and Confirmation as one of the sacraments of initiation. We are inserted, as a community, into the Death/Resurrection of Christ. We hear again about our dignity. In Baptism we were anointed with the Chrism of salvation. As Christ was anointed priest, prophet and king, we prayed that we would live always as members of his body.

In Mass we are told the same thing – that we are a chosen race, a royal priesthood, a people set apart.

We are back to the gesture and phrase of my childhood. The splash of holy water and the reminder: 'Don't forget who you are.'

3. In the word read

In Ireland, we still feel that the liturgy of the word is

like the minor match. A bit of a bonus if you are in time for it, no great loss if you are not. I'm not too sure we have really accepted the liturgy of the word as a substantial part of the Mass. There is still a residue of the old criterion for when we have missed Mass. It was fine as long as we were in for the Offertory, the Consecration and the priest's Communion. It's improving but...

I was based for a time in a parish where many Catholics had 'turned' during the Soup Kitchen days. The First Friday calls were interesting. The descendants of those who had been Protestant for a while before reverting to their Catholic roots always had a Bible beside the bed. Instead of the usual Prayers after Communion, they preferred bits from the Bible. They listened with great respect and understanding.

Again, church readers from these families had a reverence for the word that you don't always find. Remember, these were people whose ancestors had 'turned' for a short while in the last century and in that period had been re-introduced to scripture.

It may be that most of us are starved of our scriptural heritage and that may be behind some of the complaints about Mass being 'boring'.

4. In the bread broken

This is the heart of it. Where the hunger and the food meet. Where living baptismal waters meet the arid ground of failure and sin. Where we are offered the

Lamb of God who takes away the sins of the world. The answer to Adam's question: 'Who am I?' lies here. I am a person for whom Christ was broken.

His passion embraces all pain. He is all people who are brutalised, dehumanised. He is all people who are victims of sin. He is all people who despair, who feel rejection, fright or hopelessness.

It is this weight of sin and suffering that Jesus drags onto the wood of the cross. It soaks into the wood and into the event itself.

Jesus carries it all with him, through the Passion and into the tomb. Then, on Easter morning, it isn't just Jesus Christ who emerges from the tomb. It is all who have joined Him on the cross. If we have tried to make the journey we will reach redemption. The host presented to us at Communion is a symbol of that redemption.

The Church knows that the Lord comes even now in his Eucharist and that he is there in our midst. However, his presence is veiled. Therefore, we celebrate the Eucharist, 'awaiting the blessed hope and the coming of our Saviour, Jesus Christ.... On that day we shall see you, our God, as you are. We shall become like you and praise you for ever through Christ our Lord.' (1404)

THE SACRAMENTS OF HEALING

The Sacrament of Penance and Reconciliation

I remember a Confession that was the worst and best experience I've had of the sacraments. We used to go to a priest who never asked questions. 'Three Hail Marys', no matter what you told him.

What we used to do was rattle off a list. Then, every few weeks, we'd change some item on the list. Just in case he thought we were in a rut. The list bore no relation whatsoever to our lives.

This Saturday, I went into the box. I had the misfortune to say 'I stole'. I hadn't – it was just that it was stealing's turn. The priest who never asked a question kept cornering me until I heard myself admitting that I stole non-existent apples from a non-existent orchard in the middle of February.

The priest called a halt at that stage and suggested that I mightn't really have stolen any apples. I was making it up, wasn't I? The relief at being released from fantasy. Then he said that, instead of lists, I should look at my general attitudes, ask God to help me be sorry for the ones that were harmful, come in and talk in ordinary words about these things. But to remember that God loved me.

This was way back in the '50s. The man was ahead of his time.

Since then, of course, the Sacrament of Penance has fallen on poor times. Where once there were sodalities and rows of penitents on Saturday nights, there is now the tiny clientele for half an hour before the Vigil Mass. Where once we worried if we went into the second month without going to Confession, now we forget how many years it is since we've been.

To some extent, penitential services have replaced private confessions. But their success is patchy.

The fact that we are not making confessions – or making superficial ones when we do go – is not the real issue. What is behind the drop-off is the crucial question.

Some say the decline is due to a failure to face up to personal culpability, a loss of a sense of sin, a growing flabbiness of conscience.

Others say that rejection of the old form of Confession is no more than a shift in how Catholics relate to God and how they devise ways of being reconciled.

You could argue both cases.

In the first scenario, we're losing sensitivity around sin, the harm it does and the ways to be pardoned. We have bought the culture of the day, which says that sin was a concept designed to keep us in control.

People who argue this way point to scripture: 'If we say we have no sin in us, we are deceiving ourselves and refusing to admit the truth; but if we acknowledge our sins, then God, who is faithful and just, will forgive our sins and purify us from everything that is wrong'. (Jn 1:8-9)

This reading of the decline says that for all that is good in modern living, one big casualty is the loss of a sense of personal responsibility for our own actions – and with this loss, the possibility of responsibility for personal sin. Psychology has narrowed the field of personal blame. World economics has left little space for private business morality. The culture is more comfortable blaming institutions than helping individuals blame themselves.

It gets harder and harder to admit: 'I did it. I take responsibility. I am sorry'.

This denies that there is a community aspect to my behaviour. It ignores that it is my sins that wound the people I live with. My anger, my dishonesty, my lies, my laziness, my gossip, my exploitation of others.

It is the cumulative individual choice that creates the kind of community we live in. People who say we are running away from individual responsibility say that this is one of the reasons for the collapse of decent living. They say it is to ignore the obligations we took on at Baptism – to be continually converted by making choices that embrace the light of Christ.

Others take a more positive view of the decline in confessions. They say given that what is happening is that Catholics have rejected a form of Penance where you went to Confession as a punishment rather than as a celebration. In the past, you went to get absolution, to avoid the pains of Hell, and to get grace for the future. In practice, that grace didn't seem to work, because you confessed the same sins over and over again.

The debate will continue. The format of the sacrament has changed down the centuries. But, whatever the shape of the sacrament, there are two unchanging elements: 'on the one hand, the acts of the man who undergoes conversion through the action of the Holy Spirit: namely contrition, confession; and satisfaction; on the other, God's action through the intervention of the Church.' (1448)

Penance is called the 'sacrament of conversion'. It 'makes sacramentally present Jesus' call to conversion, the first step in returning to the Father from whom one has strayed.' (1423)

'Jesus calls to conversion: "Repent and believe in the gospel"' (Mk 1:15). (1427)

Penance is the second conversion. The first is in Baptism. Remember Mark in the early Church, the young man just before his Baptism, who turned (converted) to the east window, stretched out his hands and cried: 'I attach myself to you, O Christ!'

St Ambrose says of the two conversions that, in the Church, 'there are water and tears; the water of Baptism and the tears of repentance'.

It is called the sacrament of Penance, since it consecrates and makes formal the penitent's steps of conversion, penance and satisfaction. (1423)

It is called the sacrament of confession, 'since the disclosure or confession of sins to a priest is an essential element of this sacrament'. (1424)

It is called the sacrament of forgiveness, 'since… God grants the penitent pardon and peace.' (1424)

It is called the sacrament of Reconciliation, 'because it imparts to the sinner the love of God who reconciles.' (1424)

There are many ways of doing penance. Scripture cites fasting, prayer and alms-giving. The Church includes attempts at being reconciled with the neighbour, concern for the poor, defending justice, acceptance of suffering and, of course, the Eucharist. (cf. 1434-1439)

Whatever shape the Sacrament of Reconciliation takes in the future, whatever use we make of the other ways of doing penance, one thing will never change. Our Church, at its heart, is a redemptive Church. We are defined as a community of people who believe in the redemptive power of the death and resurrection of Christ. By his wounds we are healed.

The Sacrament of the Anointing of the Sick

Time was when to send for the priest for a sick person was seen as the kiss of death. When the medical people could do no more, the priest was sent for, to perform the 'Last Rites'. The family tried to pass it off by saying that the priest was just passing, or that strange phrase; 'Sure, it will do you no harm, anyway.'

You can't blame people for thinking like this. After all, it was called The Sacrament of the Dying! – or something mysteriously called Extreme Unction!

Now, the thrust of the sacrament has been widened. The emphasis on sin has been weakened. This is separated out into the accompanying Sacrament of Penance.

Sickness breaks the normal rhythms. We are dependent. Often it makes us lonely, depressed, fearful, nostalgic. We cannot pray. There is a sense of alienation. We live mystery more acutely.

Jean Vanier says that 'the mystery of living is linked to the mystery of our wounds and how we handle them and heal them. The reality is that we are all wounded. All our relationships are shaped by our wounds and to pretend this is not so is an illusion.'

The Sacrament of the Sick respects this fragmentation of life – both for the sick person and his or her friends.

It seeks to bring wholeness, healing to the spirit, healing of memories. It touches the body with oil. It nourishes the senses with the smell of the oil and the candle. It reaches the soul with prayer. It surrounds the bed with family and friends to ease the loneliness. I would always refer to any photo of family on the side press or bedside locker – to stir nostalgia and memory. I would add prayers that recognise that these are part of the fabric of the sick person's life.

It uses holy water. Baptism again. If there is a holy water font in the house, that is what I'd use.

Next to Baptism, this sacrament is probably the most intimate, most tactile, most homely. It brings to the sick-room an atmosphere that is unique. No matter if the person is 'fierce holy' or just hanging in, it has a lovely caring feel to it that sick people recognise and respond to. For the family around the bed, it is time out from worry, fatigue and, who knows, maybe frictions.

> By the sacred anointing of the sick and the prayer of the priests the whole Church commends those who are ill to the suffering and glorified Lord, that he may raise them up and save them. And, indeed, she exhorts them to contribute to the good of the People of God by freely uniting themselves to the Passion and death of Christ. (1499)

The sacrament tries to involve everyone. Ideally, the sick person is the one who requests the anointing. Then, where possible, the family and friends stay in the room for the sacrament. They can arrange the room. Sprinkle the Holy Water. Smooth the bedclothes. Respond to the lovely prayers. It can be a precious time.

I have often thought that booklets with the text and the meaning of the ritual would be useful. The words of the anointing have a value outside the sacrament and could be used by a spouse or family member.

> Through this holy anointing, may the Lord in his love and mercy help you with the grace of the Holy Spirit. May the Lord who frees you from sin save you and raise you up. Amen. (The Ritual of the Anointing of the Sick)

The concluding Blessing is beautiful.

'May the Lord be with you to protect you. May he guide you and give you strength. May he watch over you, keep you in his care and bless you with his peace. May almighty God bless you, the Father and the Son and the Holy Spirit.'

Inevitably, this sacrament does lead to thoughts of death. It raises the question of what is beyond the veil.

One of the most enduring of beliefs is that we survive death. In 1926 the archaeologist Howard Carter lifted the lid of the sarcophagus of the Pharaoh Tutenkhamun in the Valley of the Kings in Egypt. On the forehead of the king was a tiny wreath of flowers, still with a tinge of colour after over three thousand years. They had been put there by the Pharaoh's young widow, to show her belief in the afterlife. This was in 1342 BC.

A thousand years before that, our ancestors built Newgrange beside the Boyne as a 'house of eternity' for their royal dead. They designed it so that on 21 December – the deadest, shortest day of the year – a shaft of sunlight could reach through a slit over the doorway and travel 700 feet along a narrow passage until it hit a burial chamber deep in the heart of Newgrange. For seventeen minutes the sunlight would travel along the face of a huge rock, carved with a triple spiral. Then it would go, leaving the spirits of the dead in utter darkness for another year.

The flowers on Pharaoh's forehead. The shaft of light in Newgrange. Imitations of life after death.

Let's move on to a symbol that dots our landscape. The Celtic cross. The cross, death. The circle, eternity.

What happened between Newgrange and the Celtic cross was Jesus Christ. His death and resurrection filled out the frail intuitions of the Egyptians and the Celts.

His death and resurrection answer Adam's question 'Who am I?'

THE SACRAMENTS OF VOCATION
SACRAMENTS AT THE SERVICE OF COMMUNION

The Sacrament of Holy Orders

I went to Maynooth in 1952 and was ordained in 1959. Recently a history of Maynooth was published. It is a great read. Naturally, I went to the pages that covered my time in the college. I'm afraid we made little impression. The year we entered is noteworthy for the fact that that is the year the college was connected to the town sewerage scheme. Between that and ordination, newspapers were allowed into the billiard room and the college shop could sell chocolate. Not quite the golden years of an illustrious college, you'll agree.

I liked Maynooth. The friendship. The quality of many of the teachers. Time in the chapel. The sense of getting a chance to sort out if I had a vocation.

It had its flaws. It was of its time, too much, perhaps.

The day we were made deacons, we also took on celibacy. That day, or maybe the next day, some of us went to Dublin in our black suits. It was a glorious day, I remember. That evening, back in the college, we were talking. One student said he had been in

Grafton Street. Minis were all the go. He described the beauty of the girls in their minis but said they hadn't cost him a thought. Then he added that the diaconate must be great stuff!

With hindsight, this demonstrated a peculiar spirituality of the sacraments. It highlights a risk of seeing any sacrament as magic, as a transformation that bypasses the humanity of the person. The sacraments are more a process, an insertion of new meaning, an empowering by God to make right choices. They don't immunise us against bad choices. Or the challenge of walking the thin moving line between vocation and personal weakness.

A basic text for all Christians is 2 Corinthians. We can apply it to priests.

> Because we possess this ministry through God's mercy, do not give into discouragement. It is not ourselves that we preach but Jesus Christ as Lord and ourselves as your servants for Jesus' sake. We possess this treasure in earthen vessels to make it clear that its surpassing power comes from God and not from us. We are afflicted in every way possible but we are not troubled. Full of doubts, we never despair.

There are difficulties in the priesthood. Falling vocations. Questions about seminary training. Scandals. Human traces. Some confusion about what precisely a priest should be at.

Yet some things can be said for definite:

Firstly, it is a sacrament of service. Whatever shape the work takes must pass the test of service of the community.

Secondly, that service takes place in the context of a leadership role in the community.

Thirdly, ordination to the priesthood initiates the deacon, priest or bishops into a fraternity. He is not the Lone Ranger. Like marriage, priesthood is defined by relationship. Together, they are called **Sacraments of Vocation.**

The Sacrament of Matrimony

Permanent change is here to stay and where is that more evident than in marriage?

All the debates on divorce say that it changes the definition of marriage. But that has already changed. The fact of couples living with each other before marriage has altered it every bit as much as divorce. Living away from the extended family, both spouses working, better education, urbanisation, contraception, mortgages, the threat of redundancy, the chance that one or other will mature to a point out of reach of the partner – all these have changed the way people live marriage, if not the text-book definition of marriage.

There is a growing split between the loftiness of the Church's vision of marriage and the lived reality. There is hardly a more touching ceremony whether religious or civil, than a Church marriage ceremony. Yet, it gets harder to live up to.

I find the Nuptial Blessing beautiful.

> May your blessings come upon them. May they find happiness in their love for each other. May they praise you in their days of happiness and turn to you in times of sorrow. May they know the joy of your help in their work and the strength of your presence in their need. May they worship you with the Church and be your witnesses in the world. May old age come to them in the company of their friends, and may they reach at last the kingdom of heaven.

Often, you sense that the couple are hearing this too late. Sure, they've done the pre-marriage course but the culture among their mates often forces them to 'act the hard' and resist the poetry of what is being discussed. But, time and time again, the ritual of the final preparations, the flowers, the music, the crush of family and friends – all this opens the pores and you sense a deep listening and a fierce desire for it to be like the words say. But then the words are gone and lost in the flurry and craic of the reception and the life beyond.

I hope couples keep their booklet and look at it more often than I suspect they go through the photo album.

Young couples today are caught between conflicting sets of values. On the one hand their sexual mores are very different. They are under fierce pressure to have the body beautiful and maintain it. A nice home must be instant and in place after the honeymoon. All this adds up to an attitude that doesn't help marriage, especially as time goes by, the body ages and the children make a shambles of the nice home.

On the other hand, they live at a time where there is a discovery of the value of communications, equality, and meeting each other's emotional needs. This adds up to an attitude that supports marriage.

The problem is the imbalance between the first set of pressures and the second or between one partner who has bought heavily into the first set and the other partner who put the second set first.

Marriage is subject to strong social forces, no matter how resolute the couple, and no matter how noble the vision of the Church. She teaches that it is a sacrament, a reflection of the mystery of God's love for us. This language and concept fit uneasily into much of our culture. But all the more reason to proclaim it. The Church's teaching on the nature of marriage as a sacrament could be argued to be one of its most valuable contributions to Christian living.

Scripture starts in Genesis with the creation of man and woman *in the image of God*. It ends in the Apocalypse with 'the wedding-feast of the Lamb'. In between, the prophets saw God's covenant with Israel in the image of exclusive and faithful married love. The marriage of man and woman bears the imprint of God's love.

'We were made in love. Love is our origin, our constant calling, our fulfilment in heaven.' (Preface to the Marriage Rite)

The first miracle of Jesus is at a wedding. A confirmation that marriage is a special reflection of the nature of God and a signal that all sacramental marriages will have the presence of Christ.

All the sacraments are an unveiling of God's love. From Baptism on. All of them say that the answer to Adam's question 'Who am I?' – lies hidden in that love. In a special way, the sacrament of marriage introduces two people to an intimacy that leads to mystery and, ideally, leads them to a place where they can intuit God's love, even if they can't put words on it.

I got a letter from a man whose wife has Alzheimer's Disease. A part of it:

> 'If there's such a thing as a marriage made in heaven, it was ours. We wanted to be together all the time. And then, when she was only fifty-six years old, my wife Marguerite was diagnosed as having Alzheimer's Disease. She deteriorated rapidly.
>
> She forgot how to spell and how to write. If we went out somewhere and she went to the Ladies, she forgot how to get out. And most agonising of all, she forgot herself. This beautiful woman would look at photos of herself and not recognise herself.
>
> At night I would reach over in the bed and touch her to see if she was still alive. Occasionally, she'd grab me and say 'I don't ever want you to leave me'.
>
> It's like going to a funeral of a loved one

every day. One day a doctor told me he would gladly sign the papers to commit Marguerite to a nursing home, because, as he said, 'she doesn't even know yourself anymore'.

My response could only be: 'My Marguerite may not know me – but I know her'.

The constant love of God, made flesh in the love of a husband and wife.

Like Ruth:

Don't ask me to leave you. Let me go with you. Wherever you go, I will go, wherever you live, I will live. Your people will be my people, and your God will be my God. Wherever you die, I will die, and that is where I will be buried. (Ruth 1:16-17)

Jesus spoke about marriage almost exclusively in terms of the rejection of divorce. St Paul goes back to the prophets' angle, seeing marriage as reflecting God's love. It wasn't until the eleventh and twelfth centuries that theologians agreed that there were twelve sacraments and that marriage was one of them.

Gradually, control of marriage passed from the state to the Church. The Council of Trent in the sixteenth century defended marriage as a sacrament, when the reformers said it wasn't. Gradually the understanding of marriage passed to the canon lawyers, until in 1917, the Church had reached the point of calling it a contract between two parties. Now, it is seen as a covenant between the spouses, a reflection of the covenant between God and us, a bond of love that goes beyond a contract.

It also goes beyond the ceremony. It is a living out, over the years. 'To help them in their marriage, the husband and wife receive the long long grace of the sacrament' (The ritual)

> Conjugal love involves a totality, in which all the elements of the person enter – appeal of the body and instinct, power of feeling and affectivity. It aims at a deeply personal unity, a unity that is beyond union . One flesh leads to forming one heart and soul. It demands indissolubility and faithfulness. It is open to fertility. (1643)

This might be the place to finish. We have come from Adam's imagined question 'Who am I?' to a point where we see that we are people born to love.

The sacraments are Christ's presence in the answer to that question. These answers both satisfy and tease. They nourish the journey at significant moments. But they also raise the eye to the point beyond the horizon, where we suspect there is the fuller answer. They are steps on a pilgrim's way. Each sacrament pushes us against some fence, beyond which we suspect is the full and absolute answer to our wandering. They teach us that the goal is the person of Jesus Christ, the journey a relationship with him.

The sacraments are not the destination, but they encourage us to make the journey. And feed us as we travel together.